I laugh

There

You

are

I cry

There

You

Are

When I choose

To love

The one

Who loves me

Arno's work has been exhibited across the world for the last two decades. His paintings and poems celebrate moments of yearning sublime love and the solitary quietness of the Australian bush

My life began in 1949. I grew up surrounded by art and music in a normal 50's family, except that my Father was some 30 years older than my Mother, which was not so "normal".

In those years, I made my paintings, drawings and had the requisite garage band; then leaving school as soon as I could, I answered an ad for Art Studio Junior. Naively expecting to be taught painting, I found my self being trained as a finished artist for the advertising industry.

By selecting that straw, I began illustrating my way into the world of Graphic Design. After some years in Europe as apprentice to excellent designers, the call of the land, Australia, drew me home.

18 years of commercial success followed with my own design company, Lunn Dyer; then the world of business, money, the 80's and clients finally crashed all around me. Free at last, I travelled to the Byron Bay hinterland, The Snowy Mountains and West of the Great Divide. My painting began again in earnest.

In London 1971 I had a remarkable meeting with a very young Indian Teacher, speaking for the first time in the West.

Since 1973 I have practised the gift of His way to be within myself; so as to know and feel a contentment and gratitude free of worldly attributes. This ongoing revelation of my inner life, along with my newfound free time living in the countryside, began to inform my art practice.

The words, drawings and paintings in this book are my endeavour to communicate my gratitude, my love of this land, the spirit we all have in common, this gift of the miracle of our human life and our capacity to know and express that beauty.

I hope in some way this work touches a familiar place in your heart. Lovo.

Arno.

Would you like

To hear my words

Of love and yearning

Or would you

Rather close your ears

To the possibility

That it might open

All the tears

Of your dreaming

Please don't do that

I dream of you

I look for you

Everywhere

And there you are

In the very place

I least expect

Right here within me

Before the searching

If You knew

How much

I love You

You would

Run away

So I keep

To myself this

Breaking heart for

You to be free

Why do I play

Hide and seek

With the one

Who loves me

Run away from

The one who looks

For me everywhere

You were there

You saw him

Look at me

Loving him

You said it was

A love story

The greatest story

Ever told

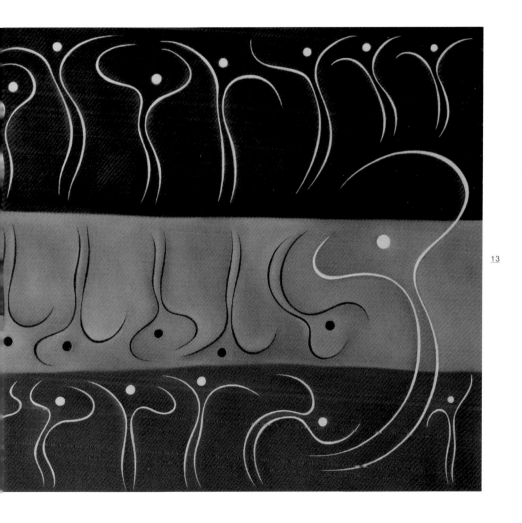

You were

I was

We are

Let's be

When I am

There You are

That moment

Is my art

I wade into the

Reflecting pond

In a moment

I am drowning

I look around

To see You there

Smiling back at me

I am floating

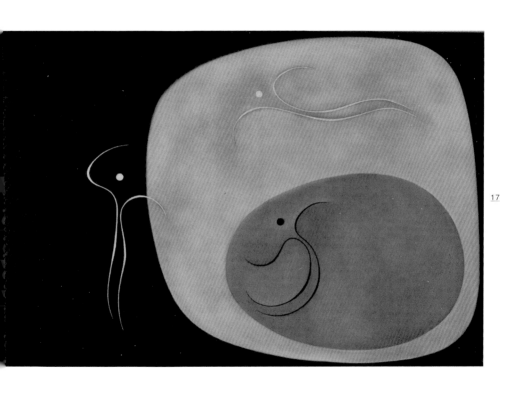

I call your name

You call back

I can't hear you

For my calling

Yet you listen

Until I can

Call no more

Then you whisper

My name

If I were

A little child

I would gladly

Rest in your arms

Where is that

Little child

Now that I

Need you?

I get drunk

To find you

I am hung over

From searching

Then you appear

I am drunk

With love for you

Perfect one

No need for

Searching

I am calling you

Do you hear?

I call for you

Endlessly

Do you answer?

If I were quiet

For a moment

Would I know

Your name?

Or do I just

Like calling?

I miss you

Graceful one

Eyes looking back

At me with

Tranquil care

I look around

Not there

A tender voice

Beckons me within

Peaceful beneath

An ancient tree

Waiting for me

Distant, quiet, perfect

One who cares

Completely for all

This life of mine

Full of surprises

Especially you

When all at sea

Lost and drowning

You appear and rescue me

From my longing

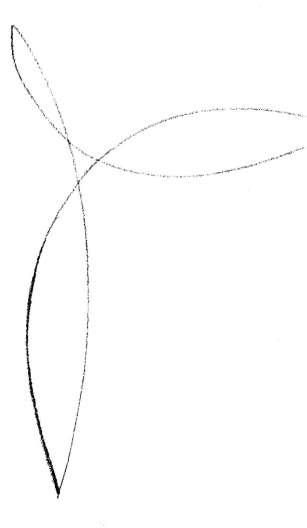

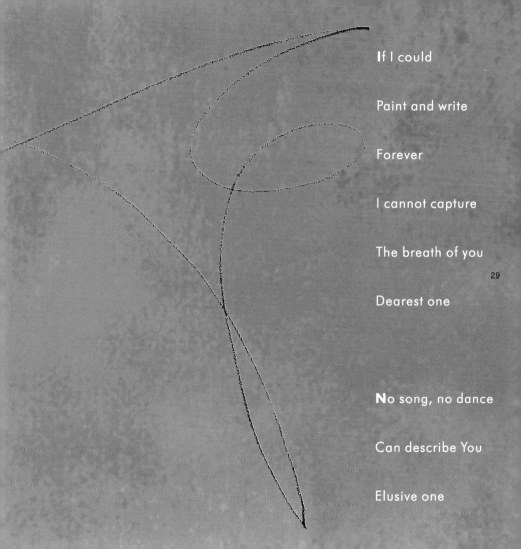

If I could

Paint and write

Forever

I cannot capture

The breath of you

Dearest one

No song, no dance

Can describe You

Elusive one

When you speak

The edges soften

When you move

Mountains

Become meadows

Your tears, a river

The ocean

Between the leaves

Sun and shadow

You shimmer

I dream of

Meeting you

I yearn to see

Your face

I sing about you

Can I love you?

Am I looking for

The impossible?

I hope so dearest one

When I abandon you

You follow me around

You make me crazy

With your forgiveness

How can it be

That You care for me

When I run from you

Endlessly?

Are we meant

To be together?

I lay in the sun

By the pond

Of your love

You made it so

This moment

You give me

I dance and sing

To find you

You found me

I dance and sing

You are the end

Of each moment

I've been dreaming

You are the gift

Of each moment

I am breathing

You are the love

In my heart

I am feeling

I get drunk

Loving you

Should I stop

Drinking?

Or should I keep

Loving you?

I think I should

Got drunk

As a tree

In a forest

I stand alone

As a tree

In a forest

Still

We meet by chance

A raindrop falls

Into an endless river

Together it all makes sense

The beginning and the end

But most important

All that in between

Where you and I meet

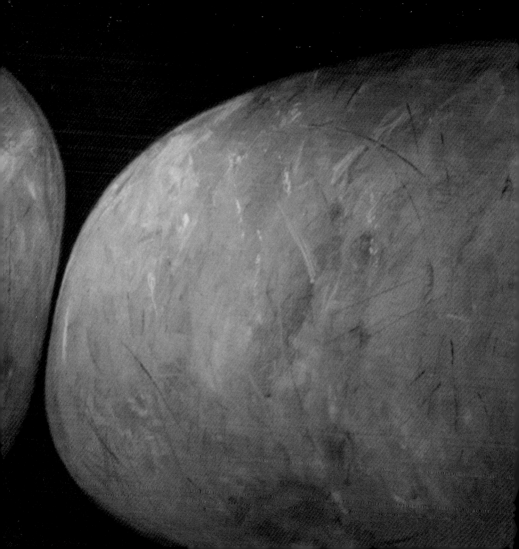

I love you so much

It hurts

You love me so much

It hurts

My heart is broken

It hurts

And allows more

Of you in

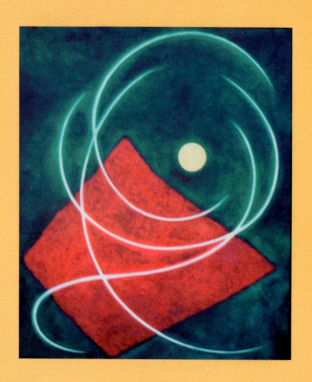

I am your eternal friend
The one who has known you
Since your time began
I picked you up and held you tight
You fell remember
When you scraped your knee

Now you are all grown up
And I love you still, though you
Stumble and fall I feed and shelter you
No matter your fault

I didn't judge you then
I don't judge you now
I love you dear friend from beginning
Until the never end

You do no wrong
Along your path
I am here with all my heart
For you, precious one
We will never ever part

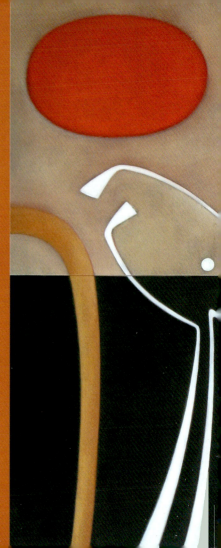

So simple, so perfect

Before I knew you

My heart was open

You stepped inside

Made yourself at home

Then invited me to join you

So simple, so perfect

You and me at last

Where I belong

You reach for my hand

Where did I go?

What was that

Undoing my grip

On you?

How deep my yearning

How dark the night

When I don't see you

Dancing in the light

Please polish this mirror

That I might reflect you

And feel your love

How can it be I know you

So fine and discreet

Did I stumble and fall into you

Or did we meet by chance

I don't think so

Who am I to compete

Dear beloved one

I kiss your feet

The vast celebration

Of life surrounds me

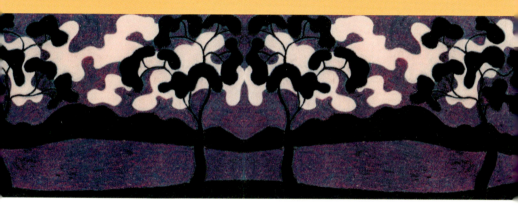

Broad meadows

Giant mountains

Rivers empty into

Oceans of grace

62

When I am
With you
Nothing
Makes sense

When I am
Not with you
Everything
Makes no sense

With you
Night becomes day
The moon
Shines at noon
The wind
Sings songs
Of joy and
Wonder for you

Sing sweet one

Sing your song

Of love and grace

Don't be afraid

To sing out loud

The love of that

You have found

Yell and call

But only to those

Who want to

Hear you singing

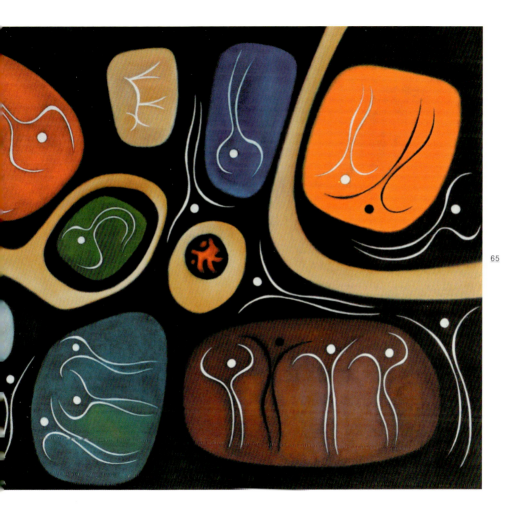

I look outside

So much to see

I look inside

So much to feel

Is that you

Great powerful

Loving gracious one

Knocking on my door?

Thank you for knocking

On my door

This life that wasn't

Is and won't be

Between night and day

No body no mind

Caught between

What seems to be

And that which isn't

I float for awhile

Touching love and

Finding a smile

Intangible you

So many songs

So much war

All that poetry

Endless paintings

To find you

Floating without a care

Calling silently

Beckoning me

With a whisper

I can hardly hear

Please hit me

As hard as you can

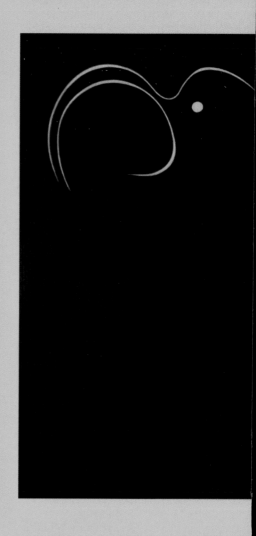

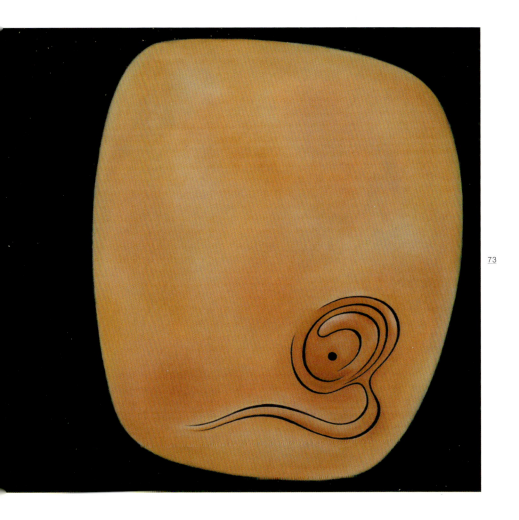

Little child eyes

Open asking open

Here we are today

I hope I served

You well

Your dreams

The possibility

Unknown then

I feel you with me

Now a glass of wine

You and me

Together at last

I hope I served you well

In between the noise

Of the day

I look and hear

And notice

You there

A whisper of air

A change in

The light

You are everywhere

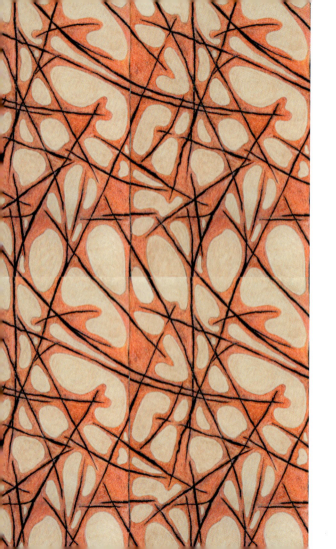

I love You as rain

I fall and fall

Into ravines

Crashing over boulders

A river the ocean

Lost forever

How can it be

That all of that

They find real

To me is nonsense

All that blame

So much right and wrong

Spare me forever

From that awful game

You saved me from

The great confusion

I know I am here

At your request

As your guest

Over and over and over

I inquire within

This labyrinth of denial

One question entwined

With all that stuff

They taught me

Their words convinced me

This is my battle mine alone

How lonely that journey

Became for me

Until you said

I love you

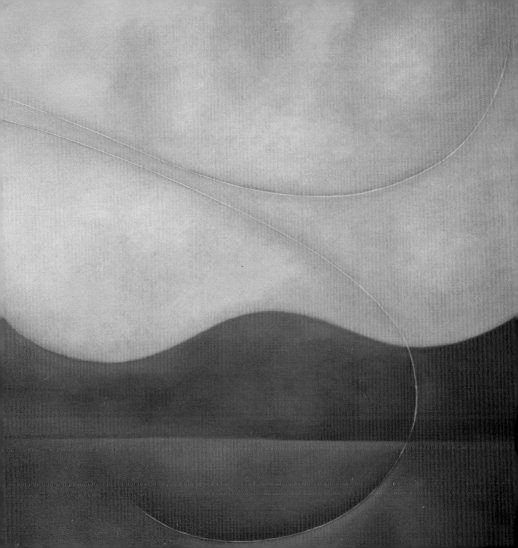

I rest in your gentle arms
Between time and
All that noise out there
The slamming doors
Of power and fear
Angry screams
And apologies

I rest in your gentle arms
Because you let me
No more wars
Of peace and hate
Righteous ravings
Of left and right

I feel your soft smile
And kind eyes
Caress my face
As I rest in your gentle arms
If they could know
There is such a place
Madly dancing
Drunk with grace
They might rest in your
Gentle arms

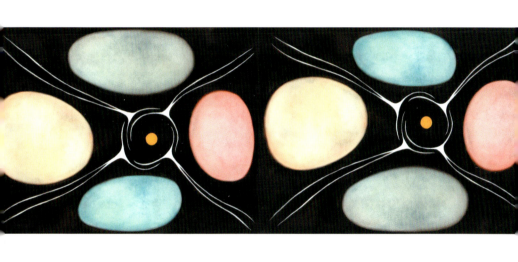

I hear your voice

I feel your life

I fall down an

Endless crevasse

Within

At ease and

Content I hear

Your voice again

Deep in my heart

I am with you

My beloved one

Again at last

I am so grateful

For this life of mine

This pile of dust and water

This mud that by

Some extraordinary will

Can feel so much

Heart breaking love

And gratitude

If I knew who to thank

I would send my best

Expressions of love

Then I sing this

Song to myself and

There you are

We chit and chatter

My heart flutters

Clear innocence of

A little child

So perfect the yearning

Not yet a challenge

Against the unfeeling

Hoping upon hope

Not knowing of hope

A little heart beating

For all the life that can be

How is it possible

Some see this

Human life as a

Miracle as a gift

When others see

This life as a

Murderous right

Determined to destroy

Everything in sight

Sad they can't accept

We all pass one day

It is our common plight

Please be here dear ones

And enjoy this miracle

This moment

This gift of life

One breath at a time

I wait for you

As a seed dormant

In a barren parched earth

For you to fall

From the sky

Then you flood me

With life and they wonder

Why it is you I adore

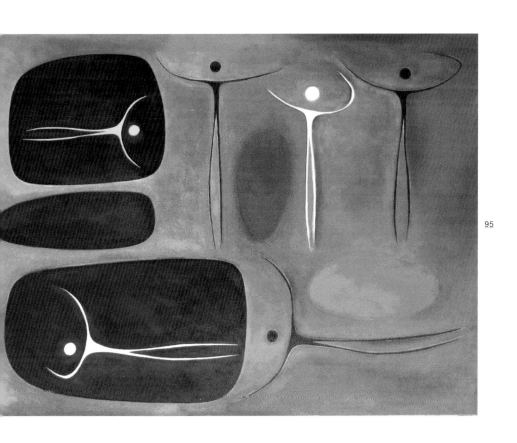

I stand tall and proud

In a forest of others

So far so good

Healthy and strong

Then you fire rage all about

And burn me to the core

The pain is frightening

Charred and black

I stand alone

In my quiet

A bud forms

Perfect green

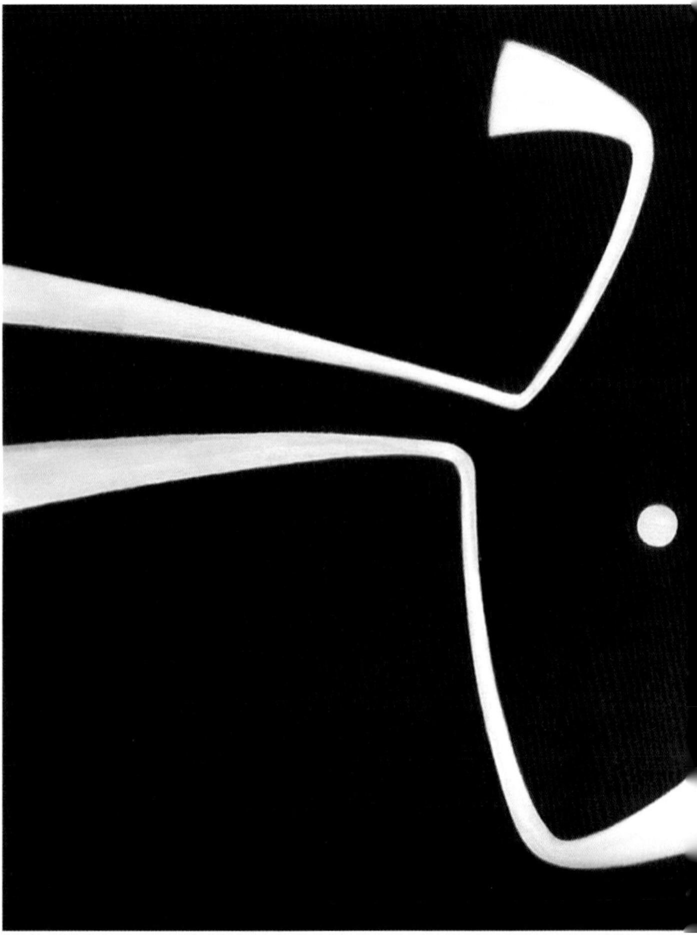

My heart aches

Searching for you

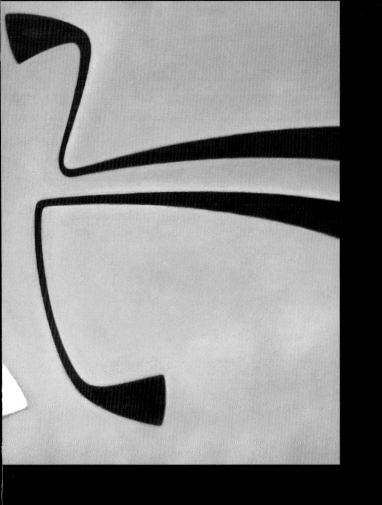

I find you

My heart breaks

This life

A fraction of time

A beginning

An end

That moment

Love

Not then

Not when

Complete and

Absolute

Love

I look for you everywhere
I seek in everything I see

At you I gaze
A sunset the moon
Endless ocean horizon
Countless grains of sand
And even more stars
In a dark and moonless night

I listen in songs a million words
In my sleep and every waking hour
I search and yearn for you
In every simple action

Then you appear
There you are
In my heart
I rest in you
Endless eternal one

A breath away

Your beautiful face

Absolute grace

Dark perfect eyes

Straight from the heart

Tranquil surrender

Sweet embrace

Nectar in the centre

Of an open flower

No more nonsense

For you

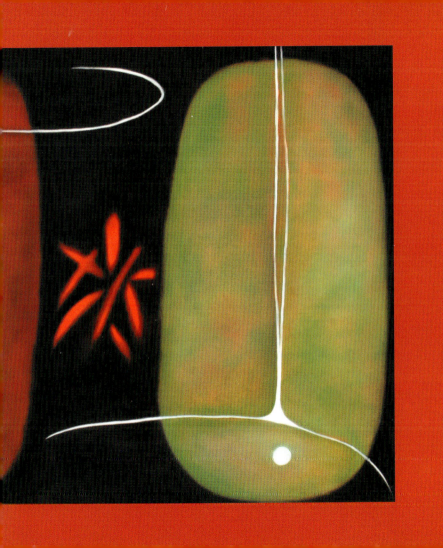

In your quietness

Thunderclouds clap

Oceans roar

Mountains rise

In your quietness

All is present

And noisy

Pitch black night

A tap on my shoulder

Thunder

Earth spinning

Love

A soldier dies

Mother cries

A child is born

Into love

Thankyou

Barbara Box for generous love and support

My dear son Jung for his love and portrait of me

Gerar Toye, The Global Gypsy who made this book possible

Derek Harper and Victor Marsh for clarity

Carl Paola for technical enthusiasm

www.tonyarnolunn.com

tonyarnolunn@gmail.com

+61 438 420 483

All paintings oil on canvass or board, drawings, graphics

and words © Arno 2009

prints and paintings available on request

There You Are
ISBN 978-0-9583609-5-1
First edition 2009
© Copyright Tony Arno
Printed in China by Everbest

Imagist Publishing

global gypsy gallery
P.O.Box 170 Karamea, West coast 7864
Aotearoa (New Zealand)
nz@globalgypsy.com
P.O.box 1057 Mullumbimby NSW 2482 Australia
oz@globalgypsy.com (Australia)
euro@globalgypsy.com (Europe)

www.globalgypsy.com